Exploring Citizenship

Fair Play

Sue Barraclough

Heinemann Library,
Chicago, IL

www.heinemannraintree.com
Visit our website to find out more information about Heinemann-Raintree books.

To order:
☎ Phone 888-454-2279
🖥 Visit www.heinemannraintree.com to browse our catalog and order online.

©2010 Heinemann Library
an imprint of Capstone Global Library, LLC
Chicago, Illinois

Edited by Rebecca Rissman and Catherine Veitch
Designed by Ryan Frieson and Betsy Wernert
Picture research by Elizabeth Alexander and Rebecca Sodergren
Production by Duncan Gilbert
Originated by Heinemann Library
Printed in China by South China Printing Company Ltd

Library of Congress Cataloging-in-Publication Data
Barraclough, Sue.
  Fair play / Sue Barraclough.
    p. cm. -- (Exploring citizenship)
  Includes bibliographical references and index.
  ISBN 978-1-4329-3313-5 (hc) -- ISBN 978-1-4329-3321-0 (pb)
 1. Sportsmanship--Juvenile literature. 2. Conduct of life--Juvenile literature. 3. Respect for persons--Juvenile literature. I. Title.
  GV706.3.B368 2009
  175--dc22
                            2008055301

Acknowledgments

We would like to thank the following for permission to reproduce photographs: Alamy **pp. 7** (© Ben Molyneux People), **13** (© Photostockfile), **18** (© Radius Images); © Corbis **9**; Corbis **pp 4** (© SW Productions/Brand X), **5** (© Jim Craigmyle), **6** (© Randy Faris), **8** (© Image Source), **12** (© Lawrence Manning), **20** (© Everett Kennedy Brown/EPA), **22** (© Diego Azubel/epa), **26** (© William Manning); Getty Images **pp. 10** (Julian Finney), **11** (Corey Davis), **15** (Nikolaevich/Taxi), **17** (Jim Doberman/Taxi), **19** (Sandra Behne/Bongarts), **23** (Jim McIsaac), **24** (Dean Treml/Stringer/AFP), **27** (JJ/Taxi), **29** (Symphonie/Iconica); PA Photos **p. 14** (Christof Stache/AP); Photolibrary **p. 16** (Corbis).

Cover photograph of soccer teams exchanging handshakes reproduced with permission of Corbis (© Fancy/Veer).

The publishers would like to thank Yael Biederman for her help in the preparation of this book.

Every effort has been made to contact copyright holders of any material reproduced in this book. Any omissions will be rectified in subsequent printings if notice is given to the publisher.

All the Internet addresses (URLs) given in this book were valid at the time of going to press. However, due to the dynamic nature of the Internet, some addresses may have changed, or sites may have changed or ceased to exist since publication. While the author and publisher regret any inconvenience this may cause readers, no responsibility for any such changes can be accepted by either the author or the publisher.

Contents

Some words are shown in bold, **like this**. You can find out what they mean by looking in the glossary.

What Is Citizenship?

Citizenship is about being a member of a group. A group can be a family, a class, a team, or a country. A citizen has certain **rights** and **responsibilities**.

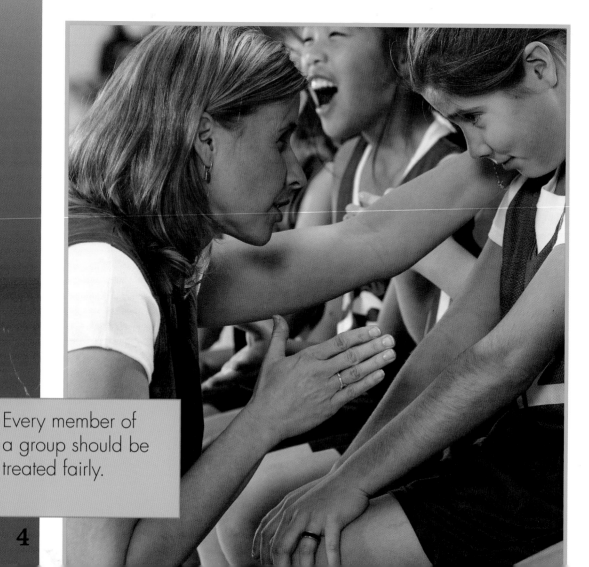

Every member of a group should be treated fairly.

Having rights means that other people should treat you in a certain way. Having responsibilities means you should try to act or behave in a certain way toward others.

A good citizen makes sure that no one feels left out.

What Is Fair Play?

Fair play is a way of acting or behaving when you are playing games or sports. Fair play is understanding that how you act is important and affects others.

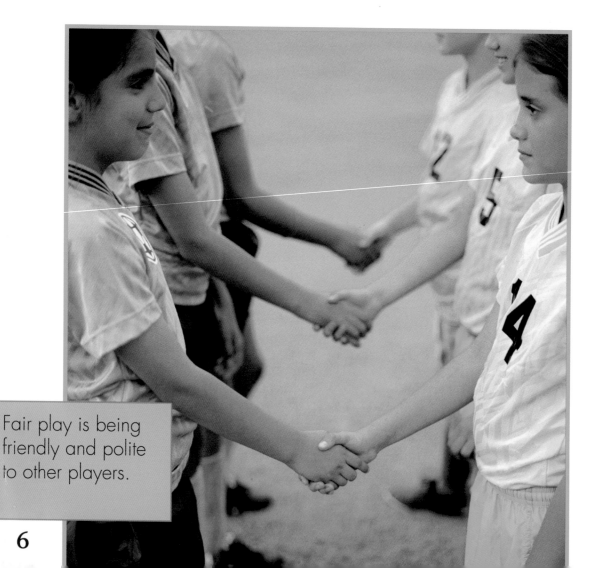

Fair play is being friendly and polite to other players.

No matter the game,
you should always
expect others to
play fairly.

You have a **responsibility** to act in a fair
way. You also have a **right** to be treated
in a fair way by others.

7

Respecting Others

Listening to the referee is part of playing fairly.

Fair play is also about **respecting** others, such as players, coaches, referees, and spectators. Everyone has the **right** to take part and to be treated with respect.

Fair play is about taking time to listen and understand what you are being told. Coaches and teachers have knowledge and experience to share. All the players on a team should be able to tell one another what they think.

Respect is treating people in a fair and friendly way.

Playing by the Rules

Fair play is about understanding that **rules** are useful. Rules about how to play games and what to wear have been **agreed** upon by everyone. Rules make games and sports safer.

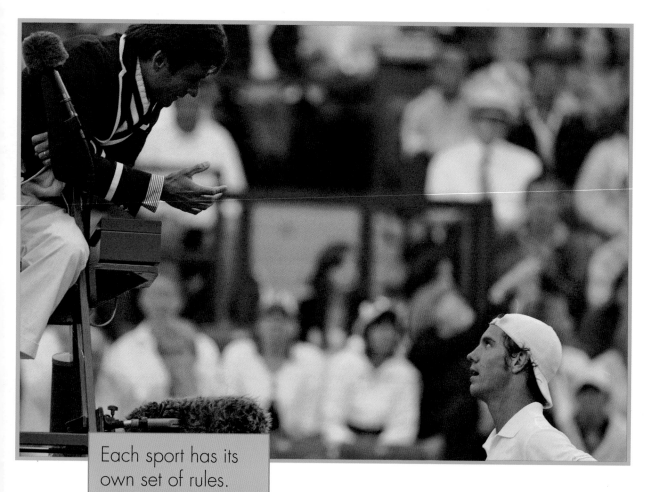

Each sport has its own set of rules.

It is important that everyone agrees to play in a certain way. Everyone should agree to play by the same rules. Everyone should agree that the rules are fair.

Good rules are fair to everyone.

Breaking the Rules

Sometimes you want to win so badly that you forget to play **fairly**. Sometimes you forget the **rules** and do something that is not allowed.

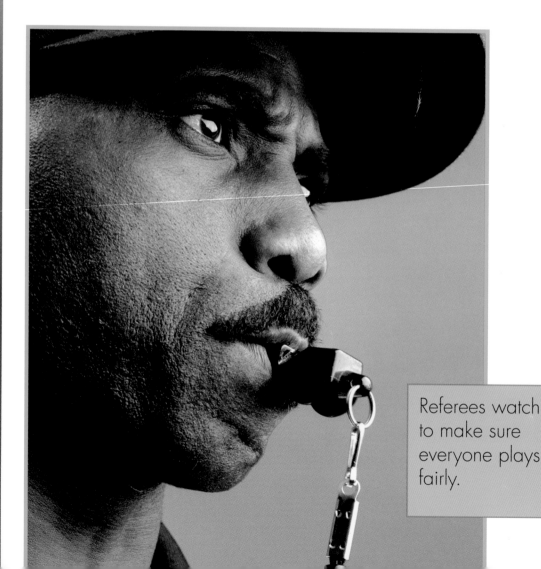

Referees watch to make sure everyone plays fairly.

Fair play is about admitting to mistakes or saying that you are sorry if you have done something wrong. You should always:
- say "sorry" when you need to
- help other players if they are hurt
- try not to shout or get angry

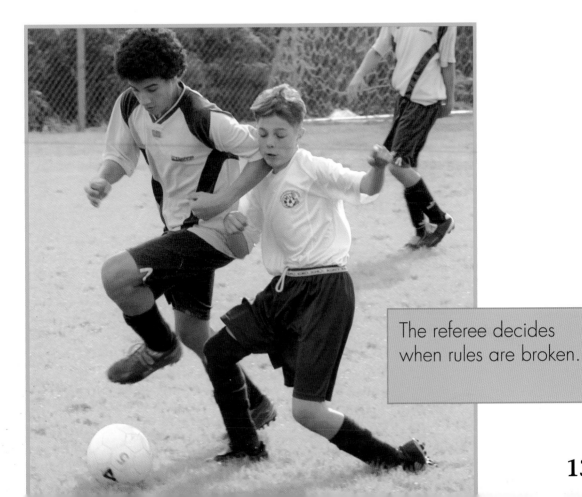

The referee decides when rules are broken.

What Is Cheating?

Cheating is breaking the **rules**. It is choosing to play unfairly to win.

Think about it

Is it cheating if nobody sees you break the rules?

Would you feel happy if you had cheated to win?

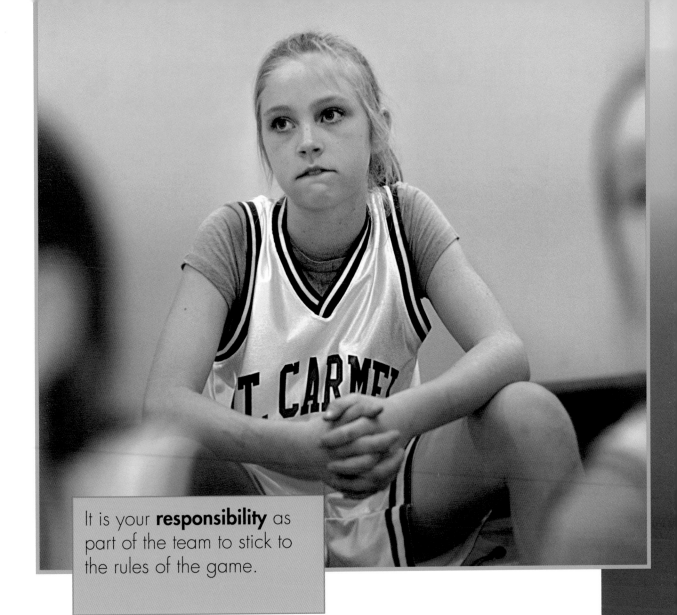

It is your **responsibility** as part of the team to stick to the rules of the game.

If you cheat or break the rules, other people may not see you or find out. But even if they do not find out, you will know. Even if you win, this can stop you from feeling happy.

Controlling Your Feelings

Do you think shouting when you are angry is a good thing?

Sometimes you may feel upset or angry about something that has happened in a game. You may get knocked, hit, or pushed by other players. Try not to take it personally. Do your best to continue on and play well.

If you play **fairly** you do not shout, **swear**, or make fun of other players. If you play fairly you do not hit back or argue with other players. You can try to use all your energy to play as well as you can.

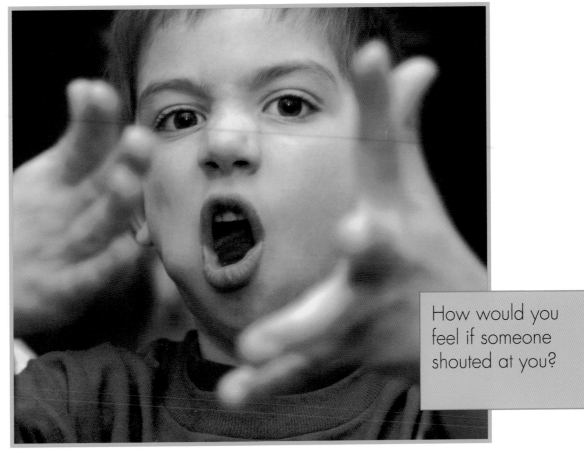

How would you feel if someone shouted at you?

Talking It Through

If you see someone cheat or play unfairly, talk to the coach or the referee about it during or after the game. Try not to shout or argue with other players or adults.

How do you think the referee feels when he is shouted at?

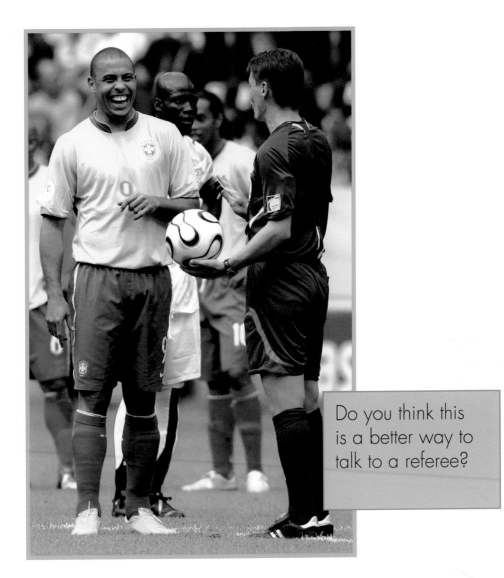

Do you think this is a better way to talk to a referee?

Remember that you can try to change things. You should talk about things you do not like. It is important that you follow **rules** and behave well because you think it is right and you **agree** with the rules.

Helping Others

Treat other players as you would like to be treated yourself. If people trip and fall over, they will feel better if you help them up.

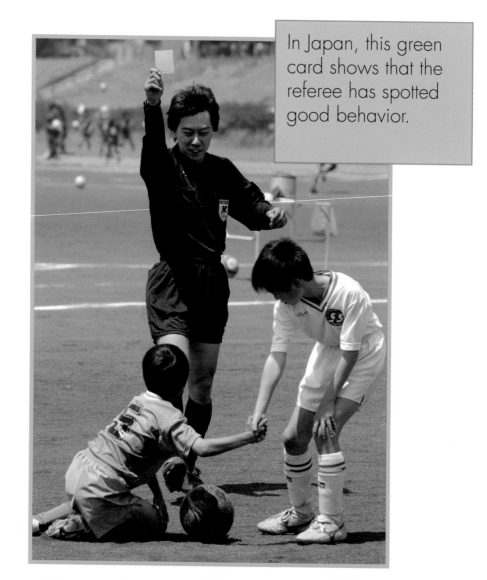

In Japan, this green card shows that the referee has spotted good behavior.

Fair play is about being a good team player. Good team players try to win as part of the team rather than just for themselves.

A good team player:

- **encourages** teammates
- cheers for fair play
- plays **fairly** and follows the **rules**
- does his or her best for the team
- works with and helps others
- **communicates** well
- acts in a cheerful, friendly way

Good Role Models

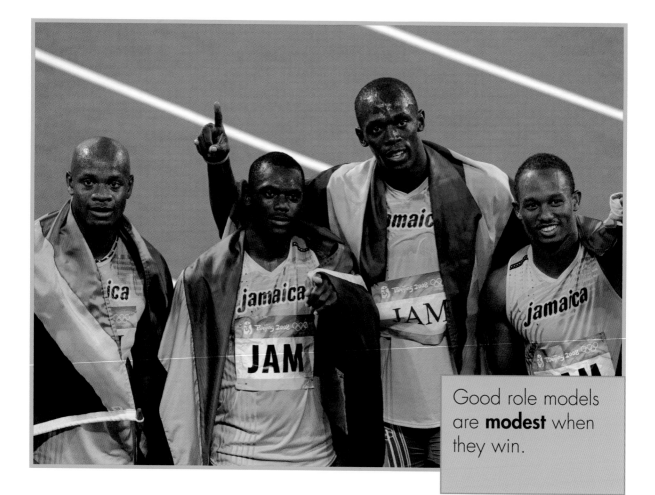

Good role models are **modest** when they win.

Athletic **skill** alone does not make someone a good player and **role model**. A good role model is someone who plays well and **fairly**. A good role model is fair and friendly to other players.

Sometimes famous sports stars behave badly. Do not copy this poor behavior, even if someone is your sports hero. Players who fight or argue during a game or match are bad role models.

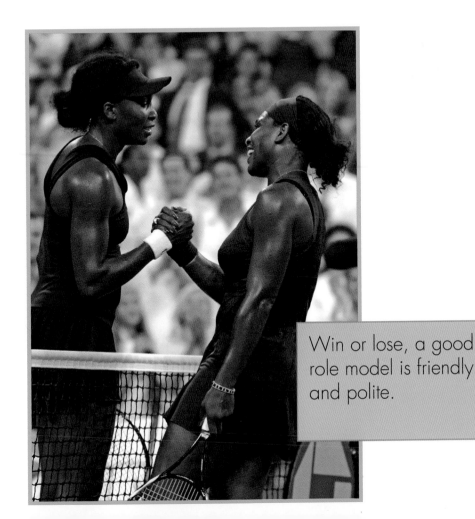

Win or lose, a good role model is friendly and polite.

Winning and Losing

Everyone likes to win. We all feel good when we win a game or a race. Sharing success with teammates is an especially good feeling.

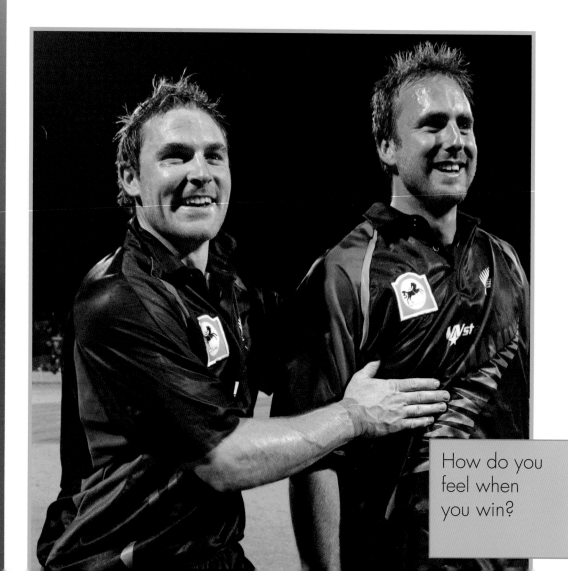

How do you feel when you win?

If you lose you might feel unhappy. **Fair** play is about behaving well even if you lose, and cheering for the winners. The other player or team won because they played better, so you can try to play better next time.

Tips for how to be a good loser

- Try to control your feelings.
- Say "good job" to the winning player or team.
- Say "thank you" to judges, referees, and other officials.

Is Fair Play Important?

Fair play makes you feel good about yourself. Fair play will make others **respect** and trust you. If you play fairly you will be a good **role model**.

Fair play is telling other team members that they have done well.

Being part of a team can help you make good friendships with others.

Fair play is important because it means sports and games can be fun for everyone. Having fun and making friends is more important than winning.

Play Fair and Have Fun

Fair play is about having fun and learning new **skills**. Fair play makes you feel good and makes sports and games safer and fairer for everyone.

Fair play checklist

- ☑ follow **agreed**-upon **rules**
- ☑ take turns and share
- ☑ **respect** others
- ☑ help others
- ☑ try to control your feelings
- ☑ be **modest** when you win
- ☑ be **generous** when you lose

It makes you feel proud to have played your best, and played fairly. It feels good to be part of a team.

It is fun to win when you have worked together as a team.

Glossary

agree when two or more people feel the same way about something

communicate speak and listen

encourage act or behave in a way that helps someone do something

fair way of behaving that treats everyone equally and that everyone is happy with

generous kind and giving to others

modest not bragging or showing off

respect way of treating someone or something with kindness and politeness

responsibility something that it is your job to do as a good and useful member of a group

right how you should be treated by others, in a way that is thought to be good or fair by most people

role model someone you admire. A role model is a person whose behavior you try to copy.

rule something that says how things should be done, and tells you what you are allowed or not allowed to do

skill ability to do something

swear say unkind or bad words

Find Out More

Books

Finn, Carrie. *Kids Talk About Fairness*. Mankato, Minn.: Picture Window, 2007.

Loewen, Nancy. *We Live Here Too: Kids Talk About Good Citizenship*. Mankato, Minn.: Picture Window, 2005.

Mayer, Cassie. *Being Fair*. Chicago: Heinemann Library, 2008.

Mayer, Cassie. *Following Rules*. Chicago: Heinemann Library, 2008.

Small, Mary. *Being a Good Citizen: A Book About Citizenship*. Mankato, Minn.: Picture Window, 2006.

Website

www.hud.gov/kids

This government Website shows children what it means to be good citizens.

Index